DE HAVILLAND VAM

IN RAF AND OVE[...]

ANDREW THOMAS

1

DEVELOPMENT

Above: Designed to meet a jet powered fighter specification E.6/41 finalized in December 1942, the de Havilland Type DH 100 was initially named 'Spider Crab'. Of an unconventional twin boom configuration, the prototype LZ548/G was first flown from Hatfield on 20 September 1943. The wings and tail were constructed of metal, but it followed de Havilland tradition with a plywood 'Mosquito-style' cockpit section. It was designed around the Halford H.1 engine – later called the Goblin apparently because it resembled a vacuum cleaner of that name! (P H T Green collection)

Right: The third prototype of what was now named 'Vampire' was MP838/G which was the first to be fitted with an armament of four 20mm Hispano cannon. The prototype initially had 'witches hat' shaped fins. Both aircraft wore standard wartime markings with a yellow 'P' signifying 'prototype'. (P H T Green collection)

The definitive Vampire F 1 was powered by a more powerful version of the Goblin than the prototypes, a Goblin 2. This engine was not particularly powerful, but it was very reliable, which was just as well as the early Vampires had no ejector seat and were difficult to get out of. The type was put into production at the English Electric Company's Preston works in May 1944 because de Havilland at Hatfield was too busy with the Mosquito. The first batch began leaving the works in April 1945.

TG/278, shown here, was the fifth production aircraft and shows the general configuration and wartime camouflage pattern to advantage. The use of the '/' between the letters and numbers of the serial was peculiar to this Mark. TG/278 was later modified as a proposed reconnaissance version. Retained by de Havilland for testing, John Cunningham broke the 100 km course speed record in it in August 1947. Then, fitted with a metal rear canopy and extended wingtips, stripped of paint and non-essential equipment, Cunningham flew TG/278 to break the world altitude record on 23 March 1948. He reached 59,446 feet, a record that stood for five years until broken by a modified Canberra. (ww2images.com)

Above left: The Vampire F 2 was to be powered by the Rolls-Royce Nene engine. The Nene was far more powerful (4,500 lb thrust compared to the Goblin 2's 3,000 lb) but the intakes could not take in enough air to feed it. Two "Elephant's Ears" were added on the nacelle, but these caused handling problems. More thrust also pushed the F 2 into the 'compressibility zone' at Mach 0.76 when violent pitching oscillation began, which would have eventually destroyed the airframe, (as happened with Geoffrey de Havilland Jnr in the DH 108). The F 2 could therefore not be flown at full throttle above 15,000 ft in level flight – but full power was used for an improved rate of climb. Three F 1s were converted, TG276, TG280 and TX807. It was not adopted by the RAF, but was built in Australia as the F.Mk.30. (all three images ww2images.com)

Top: The Vampire F 3, with a de Havilland Ghost engine, first flew in November 1946. It carried more fuel and could also mount drop tanks. The tanks caused lateral instability and led to the redesign of the fins. Six F 3s of 54 Squadron led by Squadron Leader Bobby Oxspring made the first Atlantic crossing by jet fighters between 1st – 14th July 1948. They staged from Stornoway – Iceland – Greenland – Goose Bay escorted by 3 Mosquitos, then toured Canada and USA. In doing this the RAF beat the Americans who sent 16 F-80 Shooting Stars the opposite way, arriving on 21 July. VT855, seen here, initially served with the Air Ministry Servicing Development Unit. It wears the red/blue roundels that were specified for a short period in the late 1940s.

Above right: Vampire F 3 VF345 shows the planform of this variant well as it banks away during company trials before being passed onto the RAF where it served with 73 Squadron.

Although designed as an interceptor fighter, the Vampire was out-performed by the Meteor – and by Russian fighters. It was, however, seen as suitable in the fighter / ground attack role to replace the Typhoon and Tempest. The FB.Mk.5 was the ground attack version and could carry 2 x 1,000 lb bombs, or 2 x 500 lb bombs and 8 x 60 lb RPs. It also had extra armour to protect the engine from ground fire and modifications to the wings for bombs and rockets. The most obvious modification was taking 1 foot off each wingtip and squaring it off – for better low-level manoeuvrability. It was fitted with the Goblin 3 engine and naturally spent most of service life with the Second Tactical Air Force (2 TAF) in post-war Europe.

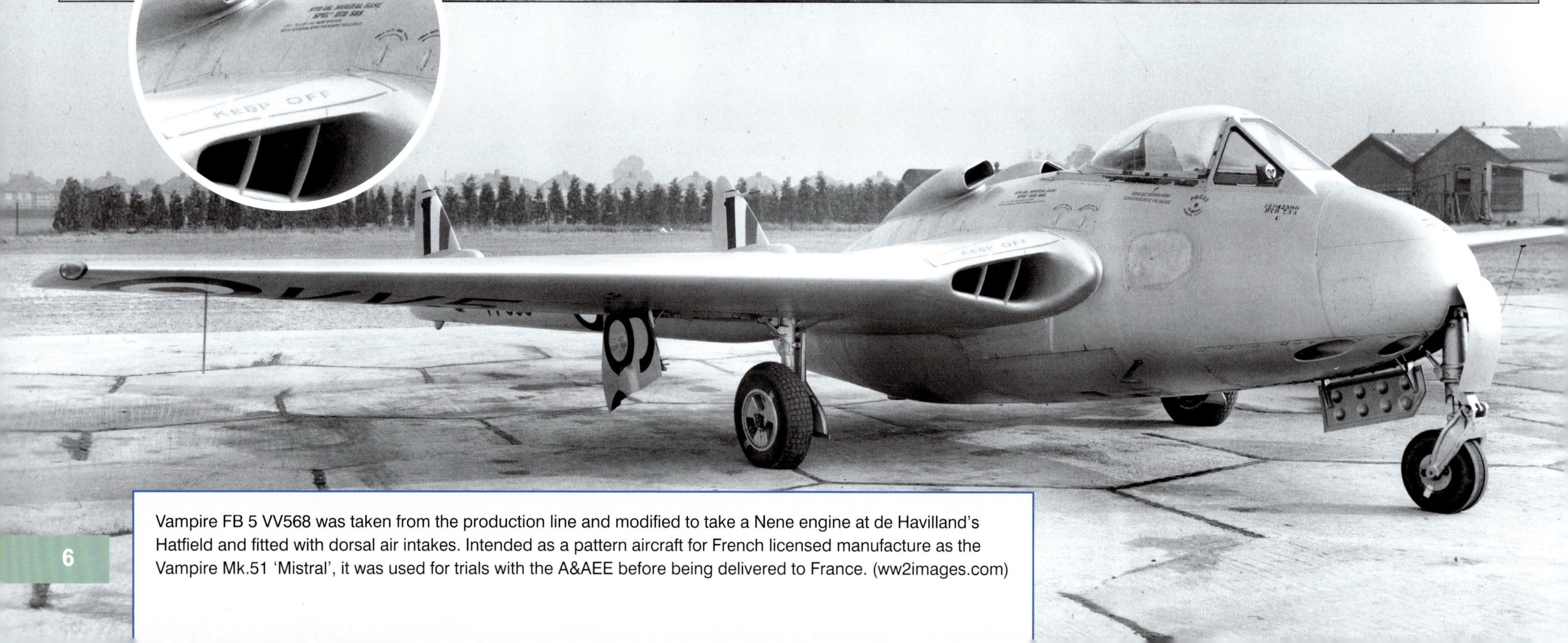

Vampire FB 5 VV568 was taken from the production line and modified to take a Nene engine at de Havilland's Hatfield and fitted with dorsal air intakes. Intended as a pattern aircraft for French licensed manufacture as the Vampire Mk.51 'Mistral', it was used for trials with the A&AEE before being delivered to France. (ww2images.com)

The first major change to the Vampire was the development of the FB 5 into a two-seat night fighter designated the DH 113. It used a side-by-side Mosquito-style cockpit and lengthened nose to house the Air Intercept Mk 10 radar. Powered by the Goblin 3, the first prototype flew on 28 August 1949. Provision was made for the carriage of two 100-gallon underwing tanks to extend range. Intended for export, when delivery of the aircraft destined for Egypt was embargoed, the aircraft were taken over by the RAF and designated the NF 10. They acted as interim night fighters, pending delivery of Meteor and Venom night fighters to the RAF. WM659 was the first production machine and was retained by de Havilland for trials until being passed to the Indian Air Force as ID593 on 17 July 1953. (de Havilland)

Left: A close-up of the stencilling on the tail boom, note the extended fin (A) and tailplane (B) introduced on the two seater.

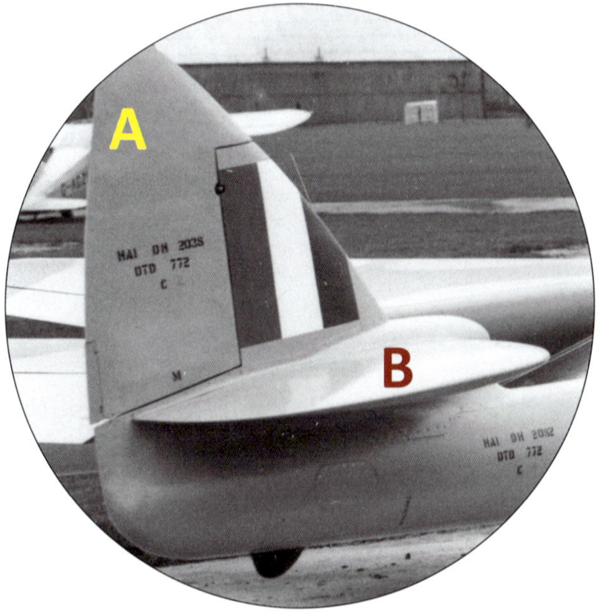

Below: Developed as a private venture by de Havilland, the DH 115, T 11 'Vampire trainer' filled a perceived need for a side-by-side two-seat trainer. Developed by Airspeed at Christchurch, Hampshire, it was based on an NF 10 cockpit and FB 5 wings. It was adopted by the RAF as its standard advanced trainer, marking a new era where pilots gained their 'wings' on jets. It was first flown in December 1951 and aircraft were soon delivered to Advanced Flying Schools. Martin Baker Mk.3B ejector seats were fitted from 1953 after 143 had been built, the earlier aircraft being retrofitted until 1957. On 1 November 1955 the first double ejection took place when XE961 got into an inverted spin and the instructor could not recover. Master Pilot Evans and Pilot Officer Jago of 8 FTS successfully ejected over Bardney, Lincolnshire.

WZ551, shown here, displays the yellow 'training' bands on its overall silver finish. (ww2images.com)

Left: Vampire T 11 XD426 was part of a large production batch constructed from September 1953. It saw extensive service with several Flying Training Schools and the RAF College, until being withdrawn on 13 March 1964 to be used for fire practice at Syerston. (ww2images.com)

FINS AND TAILPLANE

The tailplane and fins of the Vampire evolved considerably during its operational career, these photos illustrate that evolution.

A) The original 'witches hat' shaped fins and high mounted tailplane on the prototype LZ548

B) The same aircraft with the tops of the fins experimentally removed to reduce excessive yaw/snaking in flight.

C) The F 1 and F 2 had the squared off fins with the high set tailplane

D) The F 3 introduced the rounded fin and lower set tailplane with the bullet fairing at the base of the fin

E) The two-seat NF10 extended the rudder to a more pointed shape and also extended the tailplane outboard of the fins (F)

G) The T 11 trainer further increased the fin area by adding a fillet extension to replace the bullet fairing.

The ‘office’ of the Vampire was remarkably simple with most instruments labelled or self-explanatory.

RAF SQUADRONS

High over its Hampshire base in May 1951 Vampire FB 5 VX975 'Y' of 247 Squadron shows the standard markings of the period including the badge flanked by small black outlined red bars under the cockpit (MoD)

RAF VAMPIRE SQUADRON CODES

At the time of the Munich Crisis in late September 1938 aircraft of front-line RAF squadrons became identified by a two-letter combination, generally referred to as the 'squadron code'. These were a random selection of letters (and later a number) and expanded to include operational training units too. The system continued into the early post-war years but generally fell out of use by the early 1950s, being replaced by colourful unit markings. The Vampire's service straddled the change and aircraft of many squadrons and operational training units wore both. Some large operational training units were allocated several code combinations, for example the Vampires of 226 OCU used 'HX' for its Gunnery Squadron and 'KR' for its tactical squadron and UU for the conversion flight. Similarly, 229 OCU used 'ES' and 'RS'. Their last use was on the Hunters and Vampires of 229 Operational Conversion Unit during the late 1950s.

These Vampire FB 5s, including VZ873/8W-A, VZ325/8W-E, WA397/8W-L, WA399/8W-C and VZ845/8W-K, at Edzell in July 1952 wear the '8W' codes of 612 Squadron that had also been used by the unit during WW2. (R Robertson)

CODE	UNIT	TYPE	DATES USED	EXAMPLE	THEATRE
6D	631	Vampire F 1	8.48-2.49	TG447/6D-V	UK
6D	20	Vampire F 1	2.49-3.51	VF273/6D-N	UK
6T	608	Vampire F 1	5.50-c8.50	VT831/6T-P	UK
7B	595	Vampire F 1	12.46-10.48	VF283/7B-O	UK
8W	612	Vampire FB 5	6.51-12.51	VZ325/8W-E	UK
AP	130	Vampire F 1	10.46-1.47	TG351/AP-V	UK
AP	72	Vampire F 1	1.47-5.48	VF304/AP-B	UK
BB	226 OCU	Vampire F 1	8.46-5.50	TG290/BB-G	UK
EG	16	Vampire FB 5	12.48-c6.51	VV557/EG-H	Germany
ES	229 OCU	Vampire FB 5	12.50-10.56	VX870/ES-L	UK
ES	229 OCU	Vampire T 11	1.53-11.58	WZ460/ES-20	UK
EX	11	Vampire FB 5	8.50-12.52	VV634/EX-B	Germany
FG	72	Vampire F 1	2.47-10-48	VF309/FG-W	UK
FG	72	Vampire F 3	6.48-2.50	VV194/FG-B	UK
FG	72	Vampire FB 5	11.49-7.52	VZ305/FG-N	UK
GO	CFE	Vampire F 1	46-1.49	TG332/GO-I	UK
GZ	32	Vampire F 3	7.48-8.50	VG697/GZ-E	ME
HF	54	Vampire F 1	10.46-8.48	TG298/HF-F	UK
HT	601	Vampire F 3	1.49-c.51	VT871/HT-N	UK
HX	203 AFS	Vampire FB 5	7.47-9.49	VV453/HX-U	UK
HX	226 OCU	Vampire FB 5	9.49-12.50	VV486/HX-L	UK
J5	3	Vampire F 1	4.48-5.49	VF279/J5-T	Germany
J5	3	Vampire FB 5	5.49-c.50	VV532/J5-A	Germany
KR	226 OCU	Vampire FB 5	9.49-12.50	WA112/KR-F	UK
LA	607	Vampire FB 5	4.51-.c52	WA291/LA-K	UK
LO	602	Vampire FB 5	1.51-c.51	WA137/LO-D	UK
NG	604	Vampire F 3	11.49-c.50	VF329/NG-E	UK
NR	605	Vampire F 1	11.49-5.51	TG381/NR-A	UK
NR	605	Vampire FB 5	4.51-11.51	WA320/NR-F	UK
Q3	613	Vampire F 1	9.49-4.50	TG336/Q3_D	UK
Q3	613	Vampire FB 5	2.51-12.53	VV616/Q3-K	UK
Q3	613	Vampire F 3	9.52-2/53	VF329/Q3-G	UK
QO	167	Vampire FB 5	2.53-c.54	WA183/QO-X	UK
RS	229 OCU	Vampire FB 5	12.50-c.56	VX977/RS-P	UK
RS	229 OCU	Vampire T 11	1.53-11.58	WZ467/RS-25	UK
SD	501	Vampire F 1	1.49-6.51	VF282/SD-R	UK
SD	501	Vampire F 3	4.49-6.51	TG304/SD-J	UK
TH	20	Vampire F 3	11.49-9.51	VT868/TH-O	UK
UP	4	Vampire FB 5	7.50-.c.51	WA120/UP-A	Germany
UU	226 OCU	Vampire T 11	9.54-6.55	XE923/UU-T	UK
V9	502	Vampire FB 5	3.51-11.51	WA294/V9-C	UK
WH	APS	Vampire F 3	3.50	VT797/WH-P	UK
WH	APS	Vampire FB 5	9.50-7.51	VZ269/WH-J	UK
WH	APS	Vampire T 11	8.52-c.54	WZ619/WH-K	UK
XC	26	Vampire FB 5	4.49-4.51	VV531/XC-K	Germany
XL	226 OCU	Vampire F 1	1.47-5.47	TG***/XL-N	UK
ZY	247	Vampire F 1	3.46-2.49	VF280/ZY-Y	UK
ZY	247	Vampire F 3	10.48-12.49	VF344/ZY-S	UK

Main photo: Vampire T 11 XE923/UU-T of the Training and Station Flight of 226 OCU at Stradishall in 1956. (R C B Ashworth)

Below: Vampire FB 5s VZ287/KR-E, VV679/KR-H, VV483/KR-B and VV490/KR-D of the 226 OCU Tactical Squadron at Stradishall on 16 May 1950. (J B Maltby)

Right: Vampire FB 5 VV630/ES-A of 229 OCU (that became 229 'Shadow' Squadron for exercises) at Chivenor in August 1956. (J D R Rawlings)

Above: Vampire F 1 TG/301 'ZY-Z' belonged to 247 Squadron and retained the wartime day fighter camouflage with sky code letters and rear fuselage band. Type C and C 1 markings are worn with the unit's colourful lion badge above the fin flash.

Inset: The RAF's first Vampire F 1 unit was 247 Squadron and this loose gaggle of Vampire F 1s seen in 1946 are - from left to right: TG/311 ZY-O, TG/3.. ZY-Y, TG/301 ZY-Z, TG3../ZY-Q and TG/290 ZY-E. They retain the unusual oblique in the serial. (both - via J D R Rawlings)

VAMPIRE F 1 TG/301 ZY-Z, 247 SQUADRON, 1946

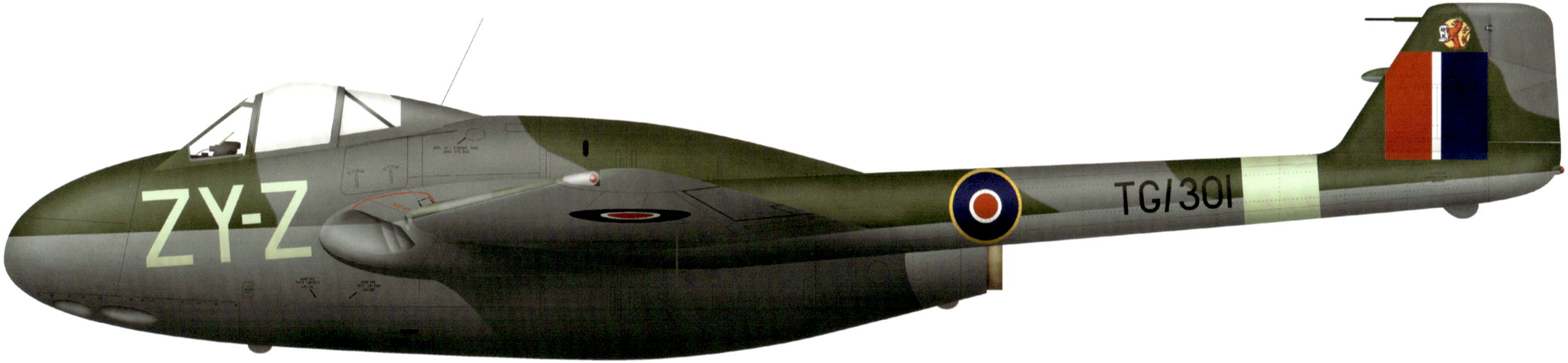

Modeller's notes

Standard RAF day fighter scheme of dark green, dark sea ('ocean') grey with medium sea grey undersides. Type C roundels above and below wings, type C1 on fuselage boom. Type C fin flash. Code letters and fuselage band – sky. Serials on boom – black. No evidence of serial numbers under the wings on this date.
NOTE: fuselage serial letters and digits separated by a '/'.
Unit badge of a red lion holding a white scroll on fin.

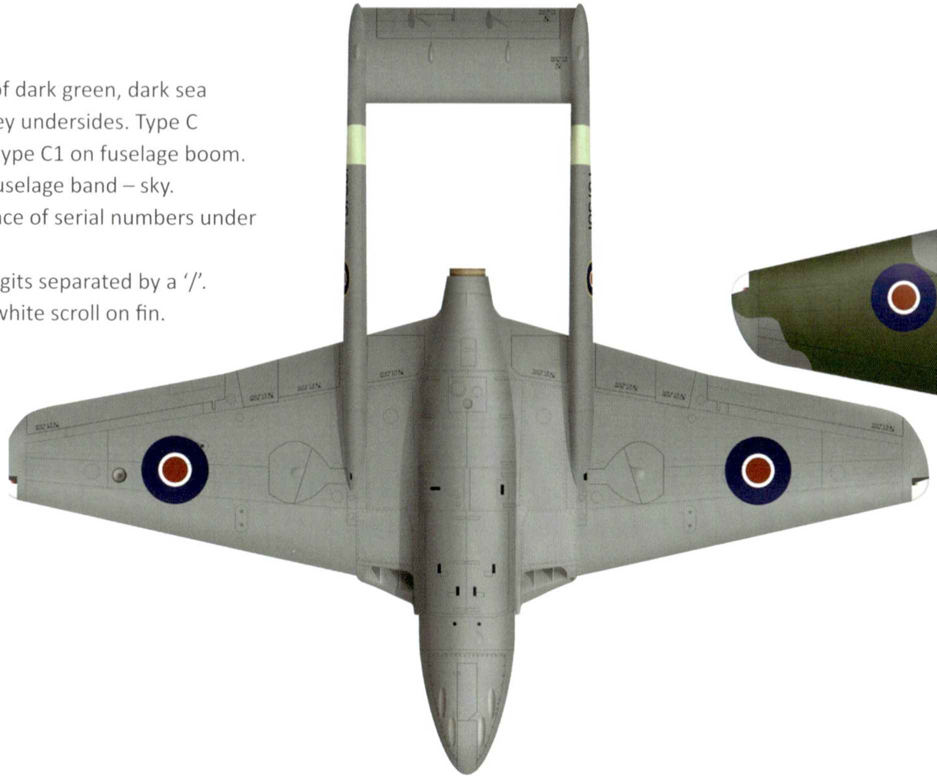

Left: The first RAF squadron with jets to be based in Germany was Gütersloh-based 3 Squadron, equipped with the Vampire F 1. In this April 1948 formation are VF/282 J5-D, VF/279 J5-T, and TG/385 J5-M, the last of which wears medium sea grey and PRU blue camouflage. (3 Sqn records)

Top: Wearing a dark blue fuselage, tailplane and wingtips, Vampire FB 5 WA173 'A-Z' was part of the 3 Squadron aerobatic team and was flown in joint displays with 71 Squadron whose red coloured WA118 'L-D' is behind. (R A Brown)

Above: Vampire FB 5 VV472/J5-J of 3 Squadron over Germany in 1950. (MoD)

Above: By May 1953, when this line up of 4 Squadron Vampire FB 5s was seen, they had received dark green and dark sea grey camouflage. VV686/B-P and VV543/B-D are nearest. (M Ryan)

Top left: When they were initially received the Vampire FB 5s of the Wünstorf-based 4 Squadron continued to wear the squadron's wartime unit codes as on WA119/UP-M. (via W J Taylor)

Top right: Vampire FB 5 WG835/B-A of 5 Squadron at Wildenrath wears a red band on the rear of the fuselage booms. (5 Squadron records)

Left: Squadron Leader Dennis Crowley-Milling in VZ106/F leads a formation of Vampire FB 5s. VX981/K, VV659/D, VV660/X, VV639/T and VV661/U are all from 6 Squadron and are fitted with underwing rocket rails. (6 Sqn records)

Below: Vampire FB 5 VV660/X of 6 Squadron clearly shows the position of all the markings, including the badge on the nose flanked by a blue and red 'gunner's stripe'. The red 'flying can-opener' badge is on the rudder and a Squadron Leader's rank pennant is below the cockpit. (6 Squadron records)

Left: Vampire FB 5 VZ106/F of 6 Squadron sits on an airfield in the Suez Canal Zone in 1951. The 'flying can-opener' badge can clearly be seen on the tail. (via J D R Rawlings)

MAU MAU JETS

To counter activities of the Kenyan Mau Mau terrorist organisation, that were operating from town-based supporters to its strongholds in the Abadare Mountains and Mt Kenya, British led security forces began Operation Anvil that lasted from 24 April to 7 May 1954. A detachment of eight Vampires of 8 Squadron was sent from Aden via the Kamaran Islands, Khartoum and Juba, to Eastleigh near Nairobi. During strafing attacks on Mau Mau hideouts in the mountains the Vampires fired 12,740 rounds of 20mm ammunition and 111 - 60 lb rocket projectiles. In the 28 sorties flown in April the Vampire detachment flew almost 20 hours on operations, followed by a further 66 sorties in May. When the detachment flew back to Aden in the last week of June it had averaged seven strikes flown daily during the month, firing 139 rocket projectiles and almost 8,000 rounds of 20mm cannon.

Above: Seen in 1954 being refuelled at Khormaksar, Aden, Vampire FB 9 WR252/G was the first to have the unit's yellow red and blue stripes painted on the booms. (8 Sqn records)

Inset: Four Vampire FB 9s led by WL608/U and WR251 patrol over the jungle-clad mountains during operations in Kenya in May 1954. (8 Sqn records)

IRON CURTAIN VAMPIRES

When the 'Iron Curtain' descended over Europe from the late 1940s, the Vampire provided the much of the 'teeth' of the RAF based in Germany. The 2nd Tactical Air Force included 14 Squadron, whose history recorded:

'The de Havilland Vampire FB 5, a single seat, single engine jet aircraft had a simple rugged construction that made it a reliable machine, able to fly in both the day fighter and ground attack roles. Blessed with good weather throughout the summer of 1951, and with reliable aircraft, the Squadron pilots honed their skills on the new aircraft. Vampire sorties typically lasted around 45 minutes and provided pilots with an opportunity to practice battle formation at both low-level and medium-level, as pairs, fours or even as an eight ship. There was an even spread of air-to-air combat exercises in upper airspace, and air-to-ground weaponry on the nearby Fassberg range. The Squadron also participated in numerous exercises.'

Background photo: The white Fassburg Wing flash and 'winged crusader' badge are well shown on camouflaged 14 Squadron Vampire FB 5 WA193/B-H after a crash landing on 18 June 1953. (RAF Fassburg)

Top left: Vampire FB 5 WA190/EX-M of 11 Squadron visiting Coltishall from Wünstorf in 1951 has no other markings than the unit's code letters. (M C Gray)

Above left: FB 5s VV557/EG-H and VV479/EG-M of 16 Squadron take off from Celle to practice attacks at a nearby range with each carrying rocket projectiles under their wings. (R Brittain)

Main: The bulbous nose of the Vampire NF 10 is readily apparent in this line-up of 23 Squadron at Coltishall in 1952. (I T Rutter)

Top left: The Vampire NF 10s were camouflaged overall medium sea grey with dark grey camouflage on the top surfaces. WP247 wears the red and blue checks of 23 Squadron. (I T Rutter)

Top right: A pair of Vampire F 3s, with VT868/TH-O nearest, of 20 Squadron used for anti-aircraft co-operation work from RAF Valley in 1950. (T Bishop)

Centre right: The Vampires of 20 Squadron in Germany, like FB 9 WR152/L-F, carried red and blue alternate diamonds on a green background as the unit colours in 1952. (J R Griffiths)

Below: Vampire FB 5s of 26 Squadron dispersed around Gütersloh in 1950. As well as the unit code letters, they are identified by the squadron badge on the nose. The nearest aircraft, VV451/XC-E, was delivered on 22 April 1949. (MoD)

Left: The Goblin engine of 25 Squadron Vampire NF 10 WP252 torches as it is run up at West Malling on the night of 25 February 1952. (MoD)

Below: Vampire FB 9 WL563/T leads out another aircraft of 28 Squadron for a patrol of the Hong Kong border with Communist China in 1952. Behind this, WL509 is being refuelled. Both aircraft carry the attractive yellow-outlined royal blue bars on the fuselage. (28 Sqn records)

Right: Flying Officer John Hardcastle in Vampire FB 9 WG849/H leads WG877/R, WL563/T and WP990/A of the 28 Squadron Aerobatic Team over Kai Tak on 3 October 1955. (MoD)

Vampire F 3 VV196/GZ-F was delivered on 14 October 1948 to 32 Squadron at Nicosia, Cyprus. As the squadron's first Vampire, it was one of a handful that wore the 'GZ' unit codes before they were replaced by unit markings. It carries the squadron badge on the nose and has red/blue roundels on the fuselage and tail, but has Type D red/white/blue roundels on the wings. (32 Sqn records)

VAMPIRE F 3 VV196, 32 SQUADRON, OCTOBER 1948

Modeller's notes

Natural metal/silver overall with Type D (red/white/blue) roundels above the wing and red/blue roundels on fuselage booms. Red/blue fin flash. Black serials on fuselage and underwing, reading forward under starboard wing. Unit code letters in black on nose. Squadron badge on nose forward of code.

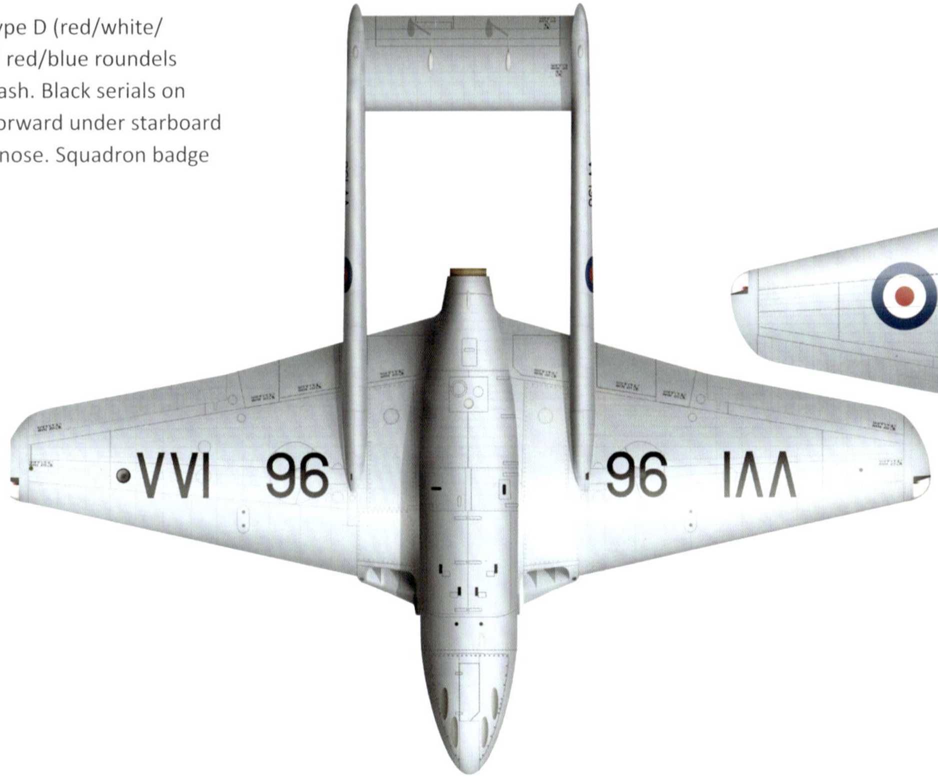

Main photo: With its underwing fuel tanks suitably decorated, Vampire FB 5 WR207/Y is refuelled at Juba, Ethiopia, whilst en route to Rhodesia for the tour of the country by 32 Squadron. (H Walker)

Left: Vampire FB 9 WR178/N wears full 32 Squadron markings at Khormaksar, Aden, in 1952 during a detachment to support policing operations. (R B Trevett)

Below: Based at Butterworth, Malaya, 45 Squadron only used Vampire FB 9s such as WL513 between August and October 1955 as interim equipment to maintain operations, pending the delivery of Venoms. (via C G Jefford)

Top left: Seen during 1950, Vampire FB 5 VZ171 can be identified by the 54 Squadron badge flanked by yellow and blue checks on the nose (RAF Odiham)

Bottom left: No 54 Squadron's first Vampire F 1 was delivered to Odiham on 17 October 1946. TG/287 HF-L was photographed at Odiham in 1947. (J D R Rawlings)

Top right: Vampire FB 9 WL514/X heads a line-up of 60 Squadron aircraft at Tengah in 1952. They were identified by blue (B Flight) or red (A Flight) bands. (D W Warne)

Bottom right: Vampire FB 5s WA251/M, WA276/J and others of 60 Squadron at Tengah during 1951. (52 Sqn records)

Top left: The CO of 67 Squadron, Squadron Leader David Giles, sits in Vampire FB 5 VZ832/B-K at Gütersloh in May 1951. (D Giles)

Lower left: A tight squeeze in the 67 Squadron hangar at Gütersloh during Exercise Ombrelle in May 1951 for which its Vampire FB 5s carried black exercise bands on the wing and fuselage. (D Giles)

Top right: Usually flown by Sergeant ‘Jacko’ Jackson, Vampire FB 5 WA106/L-T of 71 Squadron sits on ‘Battle Flight’ at Gütersloh in the summer of 1951. (P Dogherty)

Right: Seen at Gütersloh before the unit letters ‘L-G’ were applied, Vampire FB 5 WA163 was the personal aircraft of Squadron Leader O L Hardy and was later decorated with a blue fin with a black eagle in a white disc. (O L Hardy)

Below: When 130 Squadron, based at Odiham, was renumbered as 72 Squadron on 1 February 1947 it initially retained 130's 'AP' code letters on its Vampire F 1s and also wore the red/blue fuselage and tail markings. (J D R Rawlings)

Right: No 72's codes were soon changed to 'FG' as shown here on Vampire F 1 VF/280 FG-T as it taxies out at Middle Wallop in May 1947. By this time the more conventional Type D markings were carried. (J D R Rawlings)

Top left: Seen over Malta in 1951, 73 Squadron Vampire FB 5 VV614/S carried the yellow and blue markings in an arrow style on the fuselage and has bars flanking the badge on the nose. (73 Sqn records)

Mid left: Vampire FB 5 WA191/T-G of 93 Squadron served with the unit at Celle and Jever from October 1950 to April 1954. (P H T Green collection)

Top right: Vampire FB 5s of 94 Squadron at Fassburg including VZ301 A-F and VZ323 A-G with No 93's aircraft beyond. The temporary broad black bands denoted one of the opposing sides during Exercise Ombrelle, held on 1 June 1951. (P H T Green collection)

Right: This excellent view shows the camouflage pattern to advantage as Vampire FB 5 WA123/A-R of 94 Squadron is refuelled at Celle during Exercise 'Battle Royal' on 5 May 1954. (94 Sqn records)

Top left: Vampire FB 5s WA128/L-W (71 Squadron), VV486/A-L, WA380/A-F, WA341/A-R (118 Squadron) and WA417/L-G (98 Squadron) undergo minor servicing in early 1953. (via W J Taylor)

Centre left: Vampire FB 5 WE841/L-D of 98 Squadron landing at Fassburg. WE841 was lost on 26 June 1953 when it crashed at Munster Ranges after failing to recover from a dive, its pilot was killed. The unit's 'Cerberus' badge is visible forward of the cockpit. (B Sharman)

Top right: Fully camouflaged Vampire FB 5 WA325/A-L displays the famous shark's teeth markings of 112 Squadron at Bruggen in 1953. (M C Gray)

Centre right: The CO of 112 Squadron had his Vampire FB 5 WA331/A-T decorated in 1951 with a green fin and a badge, that is repeated on the green nose-flash. (R A Brown)

Bottom right: The same aircraft later seen at Fassburg in 1952. By this time the 112 Squadron's shark's teeth had replaced the nose-flash in a very colourful scheme. (R A Brown)

Main photo: Vampire FB 5 WA382/A-J of 118 Squadron touches down at Fassburg in June 1952. The wingtips and Fassburg wing-flash are black. The black stripe under the cockpit is a 'bar' modification to secure the ammunition tank access. (G P Aird)

Right: To enable the wing fuel tanks to be de-fuelled, one side of the undercarriage was run up a ramp, as demonstrated at Fassburg by WA374/A-M of 118 Squadron during 1953. (RAF Fassburg)

Below: The Vampire F 1s of 130 Squadron, like VF/306 AP-V, only served for a brief period before the unit was renumbered as 72 Squadron. (G R S Mackay)

Main photo: No 145 Squadron was part of the Celle Wing and included Vampire FB 5 WA106/B-V that had the individual aircraft letter repeated in dark blue on the its nose. It served from September 1952 to July 1954. (M C Gray)

Below: 185 Squadron was based in Malta and Iraq and had on strength Vampire FB 5s WA442/K and WA387/E as seen here in 1952. They have the red-blue-red marking flanking the nose badge that 'K' also carries aft of the roundel. (P H P Roberts)

Right: Vampire NF 10 WM660 of 151 Squadron tucks in alongside a Meteor F 8 and an NF 11 during the changeover in the spring of 1953. (RAF Leuchars)

Main photo: Vampire FB 9 WX207/F of 213 Squadron wears an unusual camouflage scheme that was seldom seen on the Vampire. This appears to comprise of light slate grey and dark green camouflage with PRU blue undersides that extend well up the fuselage. Type D markings are worn and the aircraft letter is in yellow at the rear of fuselage boom. The squadron badge is on the nose with black and yellow flanking bars that are also either side of fuselage roundel. The main nose-wheel door is also striped and the forward door is black with a yellow aircraft letter.

Inset: The more usual scheme for 213 Squadron was silver overall, seen here as WL562/C displays at the head of the formation. (MoD)

MIDDLE EAST VAMPIRES

The Vampire formed the backbone of RAF fighter strength in the turbulent Middle East area through to the mid-1950s. The shortest lived of these units was 185 Squadron, commanded by Squadron Leader P H P 'Robby' Roberts, who described the background to its brief existence: "In September 1952 it was decided, because of tensions in the area, to strengthen RAF Iraq by the formation of a DF/GA (day fighter/ground attack) Wing of two squadrons to be stationed at RAF Habbaniya and to be available for use throughout the Middle East. As a mobile squadron it had a slightly larger establishment of personnel, MT and servicing equipment. No. 6 Squadron was already at Habbaniya and No. 185 Squadron that had formed in Malta a year earlier was selected to join them in forming the new 128 Wing at Habbaniya west of Baghdad. 185 had been a day fighter squadron with no ground attack capability so the Vampires were fitted for the carriage of rockets and bombs to fit them for the DF/GA role. After spending a valuable month on armament practice camp in Cyprus, I led the squadron to Habbaniya on 13 October and settled in alongside 6 and the PR Lancasters of 683 Squadron. The primary role of the Wing was the reinforcement of the Canal Zone and to this end both Vampire squadrons embarked on an intensive programme of training during the remainder of the year. Due to the pressures of a general rundown worldwide, 185 Squadron was disbanded on 1 May 1953 after a mere seven months in Habbaniya. I in fact moved to Malta to collect 73 Squadron who replaced 185 in 128 Wing. The Habbaniya Wing generally set the standards for the other Middle East squadrons"

VAMPIRE Mk I WX207 , 213 SQUADRON, MIDDLE EAST 1953

Modeller's notes

Dark green and light slate grey camouflage with PRU blue undersides that extend well up the fuselage. Red/white/blue type D roundels on fuselage, above and below wings. Black serials worn on fuselage and below wings. Aircraft letter in yellow at rear of fuselage boom. Squadron badge on nose in full crown surround with black and yellow flanking bars, with these bars also either side of fuselage roundel. Nose wheel doors black with yellow a/c letter.

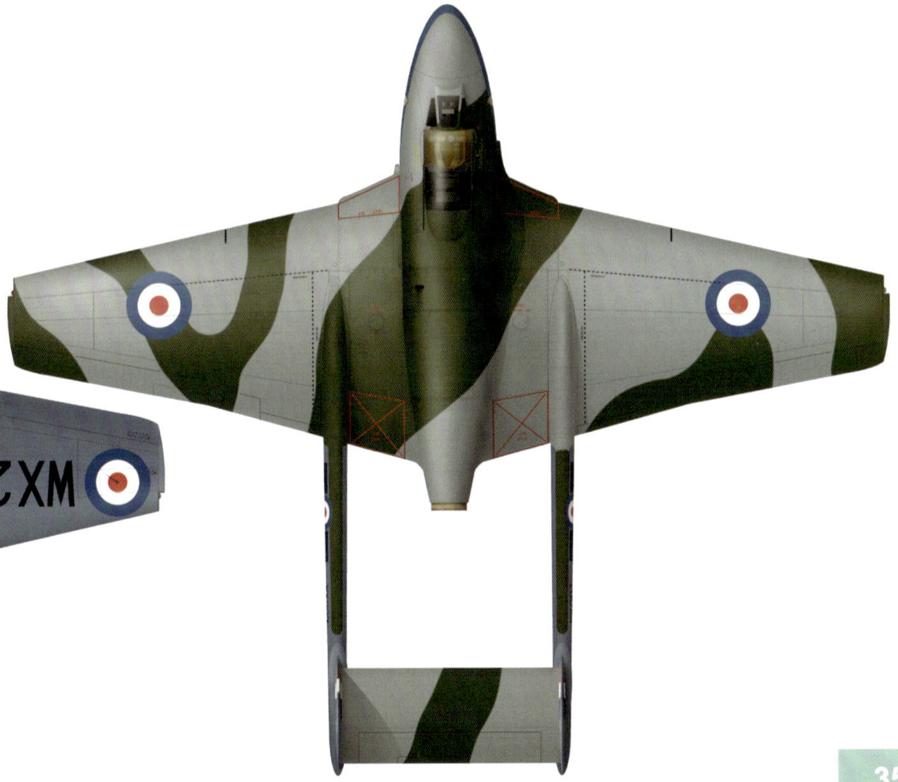

Below: Possibly the most strikingly marked Vampire was that of the CO of 213 Squadron. His FB 9 WR120/U had the nose and tail painted glossy black, with the usual nose and boom markings, with orange fin bullets and nose flash. (213 Sqn records)

Left: Parked at Nicosia during an armament practice camp are Vampire FB 5 VZ309/G, VZ174/K, VZ190/O, VZ214/Z and others that show the striped nose wheel doors. (213 Sqn records)

Below: The main training unit for the Vampire squadrons was 229 Operational Conversion Unit at Chivenor. The unit had a large establishment, many of which wore combinations of unit code letters well into the 1950s. When participating in exercises and for possible operational use some OCU staff would be formed into 229 (Shadow) Squadron and fly camouflaged Vampire FB 5s such as VX977/RS-P, seen here in 1956. (J D R Rawlings)

Right: Based at Oldenburg and Geilenkirchen, 234 Squadron's Vampires were seldom photographed but one exception was WA326/A-H that carried the unit's dragon badge prominently on the nose. (R A Brown)

Main picture and top left: When authority was given in October 1951 for fighter squadrons to resume wearing colourful markings, Odiham based 247 Squadron experimented by retaining the squadron badge on the nose, flanked by red bars thinly outlined in black. This red bar was also carried above the wings and fuselage between the fuselage booms in an unusual, and probably experimental, marking that was seen on at least two Vampire FB 5s, VZ186/V and WA368/A (inset).

Top right: Parked outside the hangar at Odiham, 247 Squadron Vampire FB 5 VZ227/D was more soberly marked when seen earlier in 1951. (M C Gray)

VAMPIRE FB 5 VZ186, 247 SQUADRON, OCTOBER 1951

Modeller's notes

Natural metal/silver overall with red/white/blue Type D roundels on fuselage, above and below wings. Black serials worn on fuselage and below wings. Aircraft letter on nose in roundel red thinly outlined in black. Letter repeated, believed in black, on nose wheel door. Squadron badge with crown etc on nose flanked by red bars thinly outlined in black. This red bar was also carried above the wings and fuselage as shown in photo. It is uncertain how far it extended but in discussion with others, we believe it possibly extended between the upper wing roundels. This unusual, and probably experimental, marking was carried on at least two aircraft.

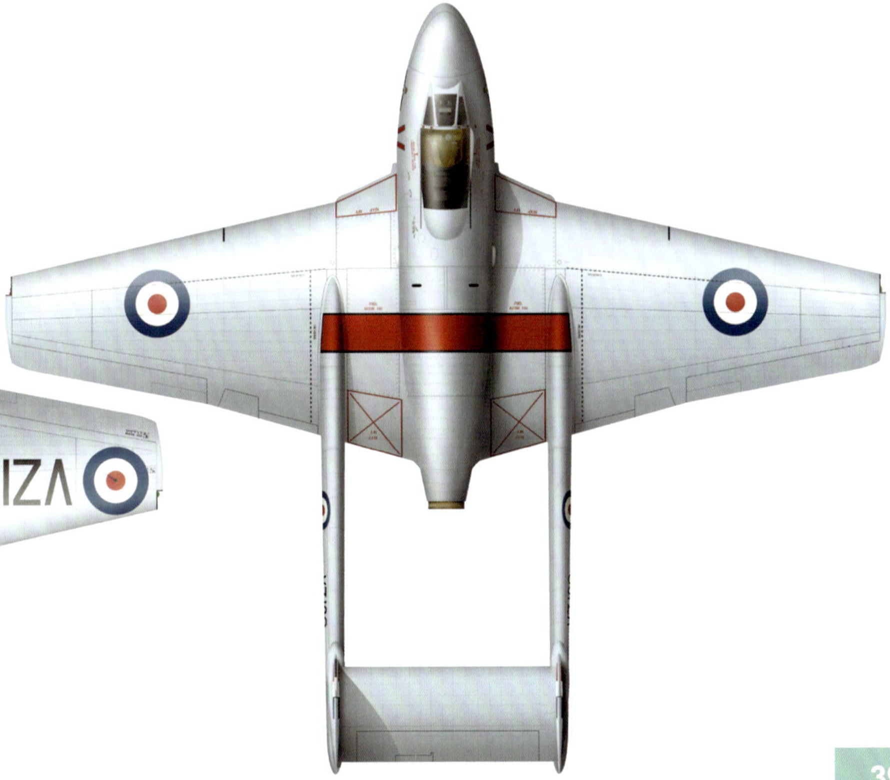

Right: The Middle East based Vampire FB 9s of 249 Squadron wore the conventional approved scheme that consisted of natural metal overall with Type D markings and a yellow aircraft letter aft of serial. The squadron badge on the nose did not have flanking bars, but those flanking the roundels were yellow and blue very thinly outlined in black as displayed on WR123/G and WL607/F over the Suez Canal in mid 1952. (via C H Thomas)

Below: Vampire FB 5 VX473/B flying over the barren desert hills carries the original 249 Squadron markings of yellow and blue checks, outlined in black (inset below). (author's collection)

Above: Few photographs exist of 266 Squadron's Vampire FB 5s. Seen at Wünstorf VZ301/A-M shows the red painted fin bullets as it is tipped back to place a small ramp under the nosewheel in late 1952. (via W J Taylor)

Left top to bottom: Vampire F 1s of 501 (County of Gloucester) Squadron, R Aux AF in formation on 5 February 1949: VF/272 RAB-N, TG/304 RAB-J, TG/441 RAB-K, TG/437 RAB-M and VF/282 RAB-R. (G Kidd)

For the Elmdon Air Races held in August 1949, 501 Squadron's Vampire F 1 TG305 SD-F had the race number '2' added. (501 Squadron Association)

By 1952 Vampire FB 5 VZ840/S of 501 Squadron carried the black and yellow triangle markings and the boar's head badge on the nose. (501 Squadron Association)

Above: The Vampire FB 5s of 502 (Ulster) Squadron R Aux AF were initially identified by the code letters 'V9' as evident on WA292/V9-D and WA296/V9-B parked on the fighter pan at their Aldergrove base in 1953. (E A Cromie)

Top right: Lining up at Pembrey ready for another anti-aircraft co-operation sortie in 1949, these Vampire F 1s of 595 Squadron include VF/283 7B-O and VF/273 7B-N. Note the distinctive blue/red roundels and fin flashes of the period on the nearest two aircraft. (via C H Thomas)

Right: The 502 Squadron Vampires were later camouflaged and carried the blue bars with red lightning-flash on the nose, as well as flanking the roundels, as shown on FB 5 WA309/A and FB 9 WR261/D in 1955. (E A Cromie)

Main photo: Decorated with their black and red triangles and winged sword badge, Vampire F 3 VT793/G, along with F and L of 601 (County of London) Squadron, R Aux AF bask in the sun at Ta Kali, Malta during the annual camp in May 1952. (AHB)

Below: Vampire FB 5 WA179/LO-E of 602 (City of Glasgow) Squadron, R Aux AF over Renfrew in 1952 also has the unit's tartan bars flanking the nose badge. (W G White)

Right: After camouflage was introduced, the Vampire FB 5s of 602 Squadron acquired bars of Grey Douglas tartan to flank the roundels, as shown on WA453/A in 1955. (W G White)

Ground crew of 603 (City of Edinburgh) Squadron, R Aux AF refuel Vampire FB 5 VV678/O, at Turnhouse in 1956. The colourful squadron markings are well shown. (603 Squadron Association)

Top left: Wearing the yellow and red triangle markings of 604 (County of Middlesex) Squadron, R Aux AF, Vampire F 3 VV193/K sits at North Weald in 1951. (F G Swanborough)

Centre Left: Bridging the change between the use of unit codes and squadron markings, Vampire FB 5 WA365/NR-C of 605 (County of Warwick) Squadron wears both! The markings are pale blue outlined in red. (R L Ward)

Bottom left: Identified by their Reserve Command unit codes, 605 Squadron Vampire F 1s TG/348 RAL-B, TG/381 RAL-A, TG/349 RAL-C and TG/382 RAL-L are seen at Sylt, Germany, during the summer camp of 1949. (605 Squadron Association)

Top right: Vampire FB 5 VV617/A of 607 (County of Durham) Squadron, R Aux AF is seen wearing the unit's yellow and mauve triangles at Bovingdon in 1956. (A Pearcy)

Centre right: Vampire FB 5s VZ861/J, WA421/N, VZ838/H and VX472/F of 607 Squadron in formation during 1953. (607 Squadron Association)

Main photo: At the Royal Observer Corps open day at Church Fenton on 19 August 1956, 608 (North Riding) Squadron, R Aux AF was represented by Vampire FB 5 WE849/K. It is decorated with bars of blue (upper) and red (lower) segments separated by a green flash. (E Taylor)

Centre left: Vampire F 3 VV206/J of 608 Squadron was simply marked with the small coloured bars flanking the badge on the nose. (M C Gray)

Top right: The Vampire FB 5s of 612 (County of Aberdeen) Squadron were initially identified by the unit's codes with the Hunting Gordon tartan bars flanking the badge, as evident on WA401/8W-B seen in 1952. (R Robertson)

Main photo: Seen on 26 August 1956 camouflaged Vampire FB 5 VV455/G of 613 (City of Manchester) Squadron, R Aux AF wore its green and yellow bars flanking the roundel with the badge on the nose. (A Pearcy)

Top left: When delivered in February 1951 the 613 Squadron unit codes on Vampire FB 5 VV632/Q3-E were worn large on the nose with the letter in the more conventional place and size. (P Rigby)

Top right: The Vampire FB 5s of 613 Squadron later carried their codes in the regulation size and added colourful bars to flank the badge on the nose as shown on VZ267/Q3-L, VV602/Q3-B and others at Ringway in 1953. (613 Squadron Association)

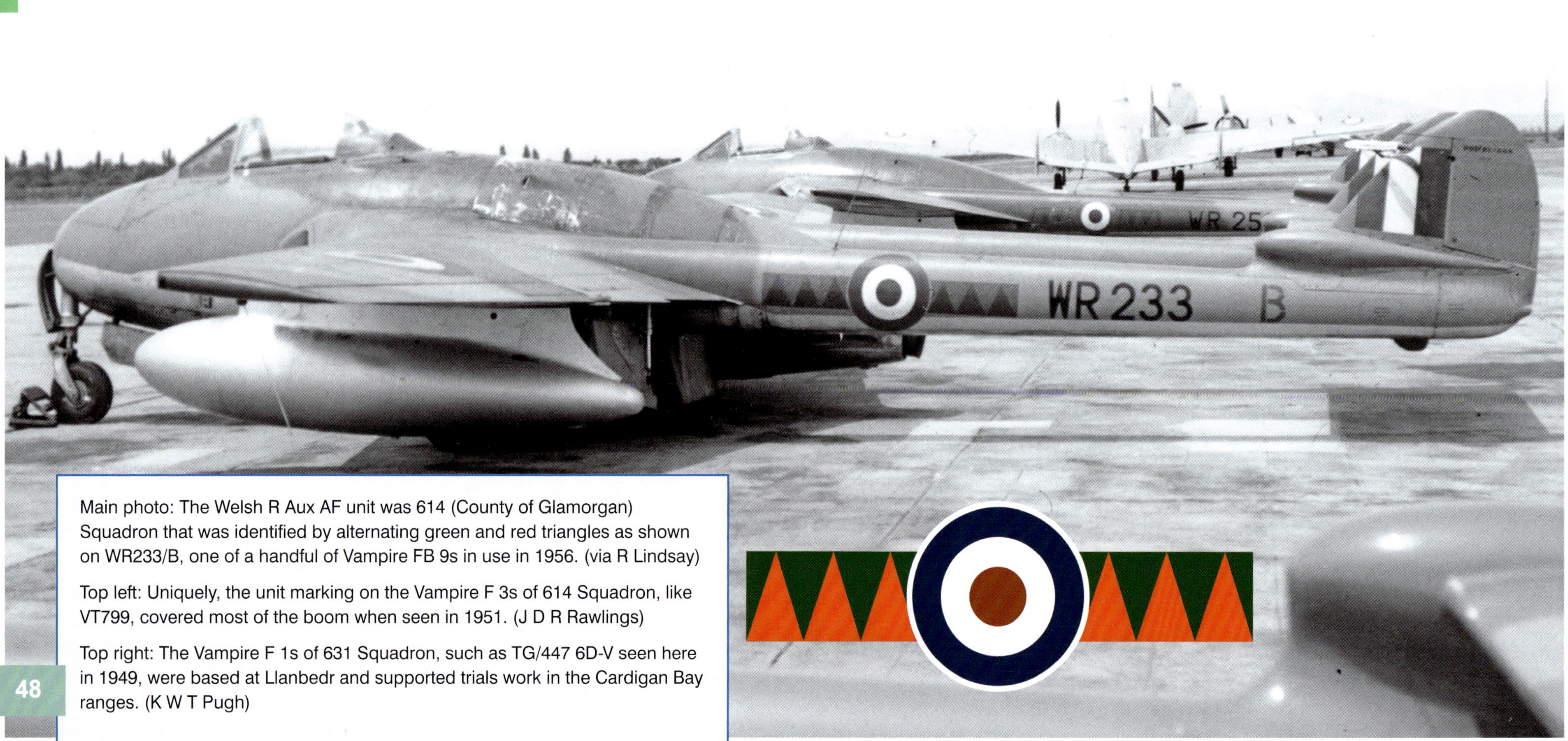

Main photo: The Welsh R Aux AF unit was 614 (County of Glamorgan) Squadron that was identified by alternating green and red triangles as shown on WR233/B, one of a handful of Vampire FB 9s in use in 1956. (via R Lindsay)

Top left: Uniquely, the unit marking on the Vampire F 3s of 614 Squadron, like VT799, covered most of the boom when seen in 1951. (J D R Rawlings)

Top right: The Vampire F 1s of 631 Squadron, such as TG/447 6D-V seen here in 1949, were based at Llanbedr and supported trials work in the Cardigan Bay ranges. (K W T Pugh)

VAMPIRE FB 9 WR233, 614 SQUADRON, 1951

Modeller's notes

Dark green and dark sea grey camouflage with silver undersides. Type D markings with black serials on boom and underwing. Red aircraft letter and the 614 Squadron RAuxAF style marking of interlocking 'Welsh' green and red triangles.

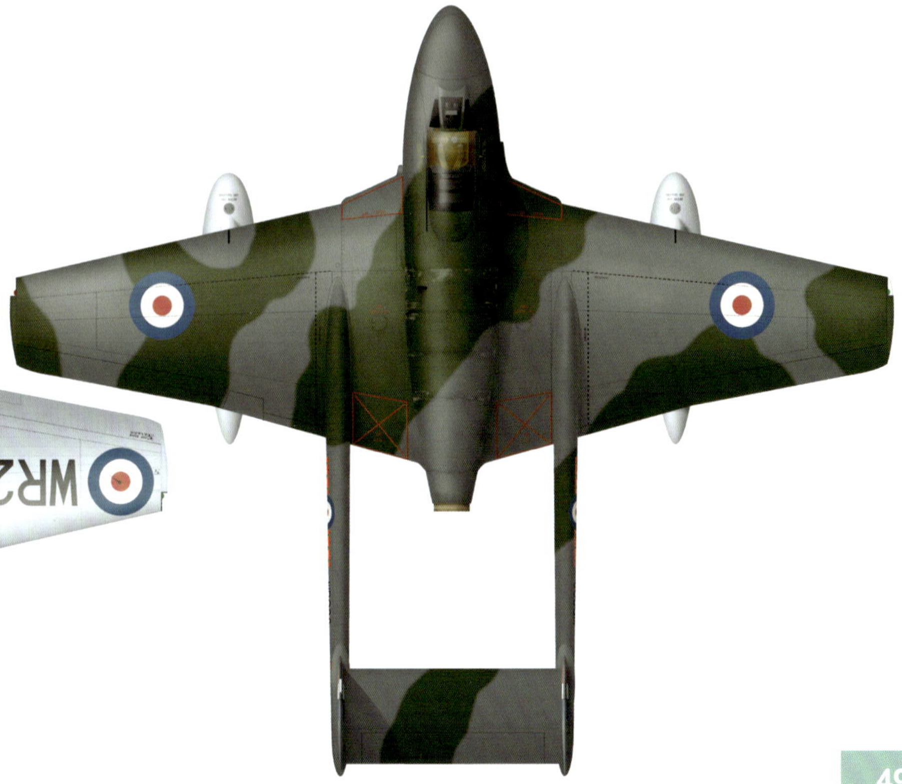

TRAINING

Main photo: The Central Air Traffic Control School at RAF Shawbury was among the last operators of the Vampire T 11; this is XD599/A still flying in 1969. (MoD)

Top left: Vampire T 11 XD427 '23' was used by 5 FTS at Oakington for advanced training. (MoD)

Top right: A neat formation of Vampire FB 5s of the RAF College, Cranwell, in the mid-1950s wear the traditional pale blue band on the booms. They are, left-right: WX226 '9', WX204 '5', WR242 '21' and WG247 '14'.

Centre right: Vampire F 1 TG/299 FMI-J of 203 Advanced Flying School during the early 1950s. (M D Howley)

VAMPIRE AT SEA

On 3 December 1945 a modified Vampire became the first jet-powered aircraft to land on an aircraft carrier at sea. Lt Eric 'Winkle' Brown, a test pilot with the RAE Farnborough, landed on HMS Ocean in the English Channel; he later described this significant event: "I settled down on my final approach to the deck and immediately realized that the ship was moving much more violently that I had thought before, pitching and rolling. But my Vampire was so steady in her approach descent and the batsman was giving me such a steady signal that it never crossed my mind that I might have to go round again. I came straight in and made a very gentle landing. I refuelled and went straight on with the trials. The shortness of our take-off run astonished all the goofers on the island. We soared past them at captain's eye level, twenty feet up."

The 'Sea Vampire' F.20s were modified FB 5s and F 3s with bigger flaps and airbrakes, powered by the Goblin 2. It was never considered good enough to be a front-line fighter, but was useful to train pilots converting onto jet aircraft.

Main photo: After delivery in January 1949, Sea Vampire F 20 VV139 was used by a number of units until being put into store in 1956. (ww2images.com)

Top left: Lt Eric Brown making the famous first carrier take-off by a jet aircraft. (BAE)

Top right: Sea Vampire F 20 VV139 '072' in service with 703 NAS at Ford in 1953. (J D R Rawlings)

Below: Between October 1959 and July 1960 Sea Vampire T 22 XA100 '559' served with 727 NAS at Brawdy, giving flying experience for the Junior Officer's Air Course (JOAC). (J D R Rawlings)

Right: Sea Vampire F 20 VV140 leading VV141, probably when with 703 NAS in 1950. (ww2images.com)

The first of a batch of 30 Sea Vampire F 20s, VV136 was initially used by C Squadron, A&AEE, for deck landing assessment and later with the Handling Squadron for producing pilot's notes. The arrestor hook housing is well shown, as is the then standard RN fighter scheme of extra dark sea grey top surfaces with sky undersides.

Service	Mark/s	Squadron/s	Dates
Royal Australian Air Force	FB 9±, F 30+, FB 31+, T 33+, T 35+	21, 22, 23, 24, 25, 75, 76	1949-1970
Royal Australian Navy	T 34+	723, 724	1954-1966
Royal Canadian Air Force	F 1, F 3	400, 401, 402, 410, 411, 421, 438, 441, 442,	1947-1958
Indian Air Force	F 3, T 11, FB 52^, T 55^, PR 55, NF 54	1, 3, 7, 8, 10, 15, 17, 20, 24, 27, 37, 45, 51, 101, 108, 220, 221, 222	1950-c 1975
Royal New Zealand Air Force	FB 5, FB 9±, FB 52, 55	14, 75	1950-1971
Royal Rhodesian Air Force*	FB 9, T 11, FB 52, T 55	1, 2, 6	1953-1981
South African Air Force	FB 5, FB 9, FB 52, T 55	1, 2	1950-1980

COMMONWEALTH AIR FORCES

\+ *Licence built by Commonwealth Aircraft Corporation*

^ *Most Licence built by Hindustan Aircraft Ltd*

± *Leased from RAF*

* *Later Air Force of Zimbabwe*

The Royal Canadian Air Force was an early customer for the Vampire, with 85 F 3s being delivered from 1947. They flew operationally with two Regular and six Auxiliary Squadrons until replaced by Sabres in 1952. They continued to be used extensively by training and support units before being finally withdrawn 1958. Vampire F 3 17021/GO of the Flying Instructor's School is seen on 6 January 1953. (DND/RCAF)

INDIAN AIR FORCE

The first Vampires for the RIAF were a trio of F 3s delivered in 1948. 39 British built FB 52s followed between 1949 and 1952. A further 247 aircraft were then built under licence by Hindustan Aircraft Limited (HAL). From 1953, 53 T 55s were delivered to the IAF from the UK, followed by 60 more made in India, with further second-hand examples being purchased; at least five were modified for recce duties as the PR 55. Finally, in 1954, the IAF took delivery of 18 refurbished NF 54s with a dozen more three years later. All Indian aircraft had been withdrawn by 1975.

Top left: Vampire FB 52 IB1695 of 3 Squadron IAF at Ambala in the early 1950s. (Vikram Singh)

Centre left: Vampire NF 54 ID1605 in the UK awaiting delivery to the IAF in 1954. (de Havilland)

Top right: Vampire NF 54s ID693, ID609 (with winged dagger badge) and ID697 of 10 Squadron IAF at Palam in 1958 (IAF)

JET versus JET

The Vampire was the first jet fighter operated by the Indian Air Force. but by the time that hostilities broke out with Pakistan in September 1965 only No. 45 Squadron was operational. Other Vampires were flown by 220 Squadron that functioned as a jet Operational Conversion Unit. A few others were flown in the photo recce role with 108 Squadron. When hostilities were becoming imminent, some aircraft and pilots of 220 Squadron reinforced 45 Squadron at Pathankot under Squadron Leader Dhar.

On 1 September, when Indian troops came under pressure from a Pakistani armoured thrust, an urgent request was made for air support to slow the advance. A quartet of Vampire FB 52s from the reinforced 45 Squadron took off, headed over Chamb, and attacked the Pakistani armour in the face of heavy ground fire. The Vampire flown by Flight Lieutenant Pathak was hit and he was forced to bale out. As the remaining three Vampires pulled away they were engaged by Pakistani Air Force F-86F Sabres that were equipped with Sidewinder missiles. All three of the Indian Vampires were shot down and the pilots, Squadron Leader Baghwagar, Flight Lieutenant Bharadwaj and Flight Lieutenant Joshi, were killed.

Although they had helped in blunting the advance, the Vampires were withdrawn from the front for point air defence in the rear areas. A reconnaissance Vampire of 108 Squadron was also destroyed in a strafing attack on 10 September in which its pilot Squadron Leader Marstone was killed.

The Royal Australian Air Force ordered a Nene powered variant built under licence by CAC (Commonwealth Aircraft Corporation) with 57 F 30s and 23 FB 31s being delivered. CAC also built 36 T 33 trainers and five T 34s for the Royal Australian Navy. CAC later delivered 68 more Vampire T 35s to the RAAF.

Main photo: Vampire T 55 A79-661 of the Central Flying School, East Sale, early 1960s. (N Weeding via R C B Ashworth)

Left: Vampire T 34A A79-842/NW 877 was issued to the Royal Australian Navy with which it overshot a landing at Nowra, NSW on 31 August 1959, but it was later repaired. (Royal Australian Navy)

Top left: Nene powered Vampire F 30 A79-321 leads a formation of 21 (City of Melbourne) Squadron RAAF during the early 1950s. The extra air intakes were found to cause difficulty recovering from dives above Mach 0.75, so they were repositioned underneath. That helped solve the problem, but the engines then sucked in rubbish on the ground and damaged the engines. (RAAF)

Top right: After being grounded, Vampire F 30 A-1-10, formerly A79-165, was used for technical training by 24 (City of Adelaide) Squadron RAAF at Edinburgh, SA in November 1966. (N Weeding via R C B Ashworth)

ROYAL CANADIAN AIR FORCE

A neat formation of Vampire F 3s, 17067/BQ-067, 17065/BQ-065, 17078/BQ-078 and 17002/BQ-002 of 438 (City of Montreal) Squadron RCAF on 25 August 1955. (DND/RCAF)

Vampire F 3 17007/R of the 410 Squadron 'Blue Devils' aerobatic team at St Hubert in 1949. (L Milberry)

VAMPIRE F 3 17007, BLUE DEVILS, CANADA 1949

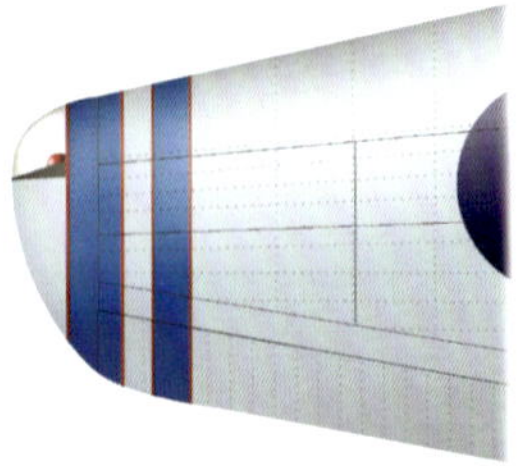

Modeller's notes

Natural metal/silver overall with blue/red 'maple leaf' roundels on fuselage and above wings. Type C fin flash. Black serial on boom. Medium blue nose and stripe thinly outlined in red extending down fuselage to tail. Red leaping cougar (Squadron badge) under cockpit. Black aircraft letter on nose wheel door. No underwing markings.
Two blue wingtip stripes added at one point (inset view)

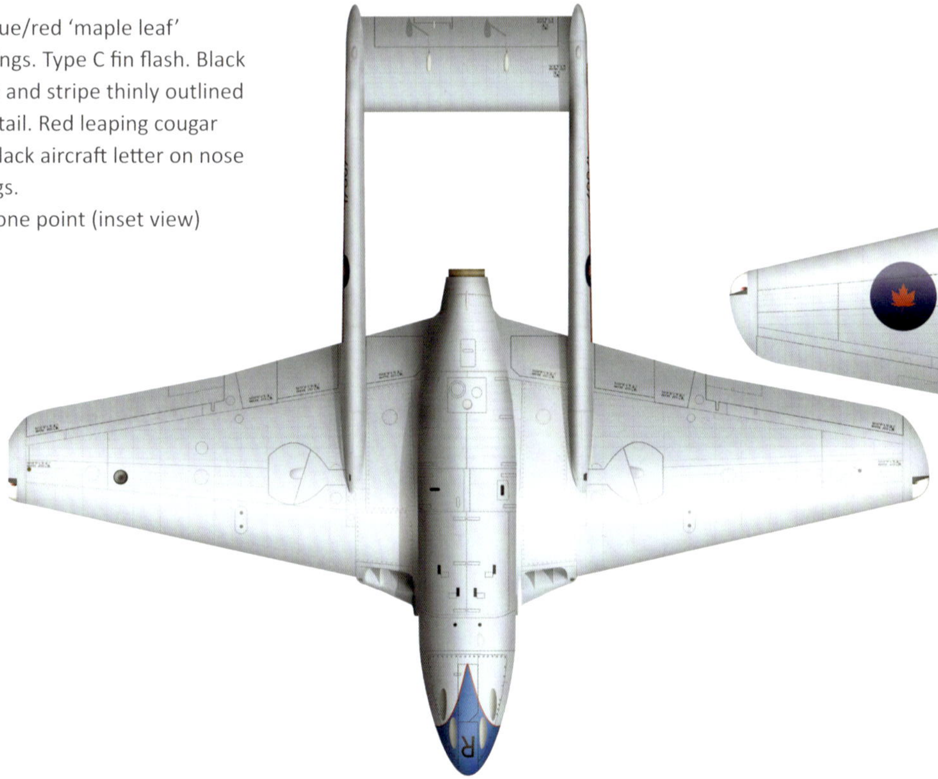

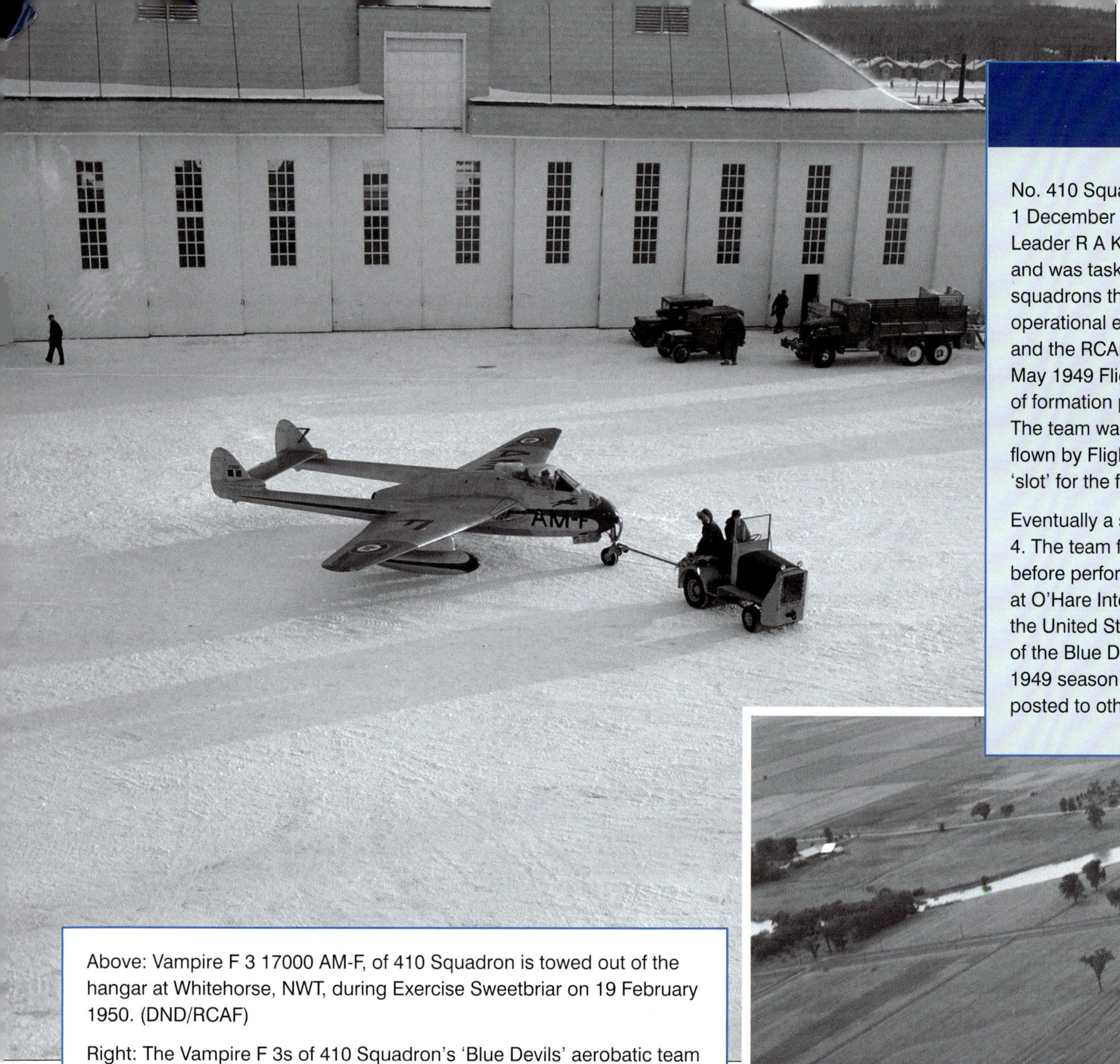

THE BLUE DEVILS

No. 410 Squadron was the first in the RCAF to receive jet fighters when, on 1 December 1948, it was reformed at St Hubert, Quebec under Squadron Leader R A Kipp. It received the first Vampire F Mk.3s to enter Canadian service and was tasked to develop tactics and procedures using the new jet for the squadrons that would follow and to establish the boundaries of the Vampire's operational envelope. The advent of jets created widespread interest in Canada and the RCAF wished to display its advanced new aircraft to the public. On 4 May 1949 Flight Lieutenant Don Laubman was instructed to develop a routine of formation pairs aerobatics and soon afterwards a third aircraft was added. The team was named 'the Blue Devils'. In early June a fourth aircraft was added flown by Flight Lieutenant Joe Schulz to perform a solo display, then join in the 'slot' for the formations.

Eventually a second solo was added and a permanent 'slot' member as No. 4. The team flew local airshows at Trenton and Drummondville during June before performing to great acclaim on 3 and 4 July at the National Air Fair held at O'Hare International Airport, Chicago, that was one of the major airshows in the United States. In front of 145,000 spectators the specially painted Vampires of the Blue Devils stole the show. The team performed 26 shows during the 1949 season and by the time the team disbanded in 1951, when the pilots were posted to other squadrons, the 'Blue Devils' had performed at 45 shows.

Above: Vampire F 3 17000 AM-F, of 410 Squadron is towed out of the hangar at Whitehorse, NWT, during Exercise Sweetbriar on 19 February 1950. (DND/RCAF)

Right: The Vampire F 3s of 410 Squadron's 'Blue Devils' aerobatic team were natural metal overall and wore blue/red 'maple leaf' roundels with a Type C fin flash. The team's aircraft carried a medium blue nose and stripe thinly outlined in red that extended along the fuselage boom. The Squadron's red leaping cougar badge was also worn.

Top left: Vampire F 3s of 411 (County of York) Squadron at Downsview in 1952 show the change of markings with 17040/AN-T still in codes that have been replaced by the badge on the nearest one. (DND/RCAF)

Centre left: Vampire F 3 17075/BU-V and 17075/BU-X of 442 (City of Vancouver) Squadron with shark mouth markings. (442 Sqn records)

Bottom right: In the snow at Whitehorse, NWT, on 19 February 1950 Vampire F 3 17063/AM-P of 410 Squadron was participating in Exercise Sweetbriar. (DND/RCAF)

RCAF VAMPIRE UNIT CODES

CODE	UNIT	TYPE	DATES USED	EXAMPLE
AA	400	Vampire F 3	3.48-11.51	17051/AA-P
AB	401	Vampire F 3	3.48-2.56	17017/AB-A
AC	402	Vampire F 3	4.48-11.50	17059/AC-P
AM	410	Vampire F 3	12.48-5.51	17063/AM-P
AN	411	Vampire F 3	7.51-11.55	17042/AN-T
AX	421	Vampire F 3	9.49-12.50	17030/AX-C
BQ	438	Vampire F 3	4.48-9.53	17067/BQ-067
BT	441	Vampire F 3	3.51-6.51	17067/BT-O
BU	442	Vampire F 3	4.48-c6.52	17075/BU-Y
FB	CEPE	Vampire F 3	52-53	17007/FB-R
GJ	1(F) OTU	Vampire F 3	48-50	17028/ GJ-G
SL	442	Vampire F 3	53-56	17074/SL-074

ROYAL NEW ZEALAND AIR FORCE

Main photo: Seen at Ohakea in 1956, Vampire FB 5s NZ5761, NZ5757 and others of 75 Squadron RNZAF are prepared for their next sortie. The nearest aircraft appears to be partially camouflaged. (RNZAF)

Inset: With their booms removed and stored above the wings, so they resemble the 'push-me-pull-you', Vampire FB 5 NZ5758 and NZ5769 are still in their 14 Squadron RNZAF markings when in use at 4 TTS Woodbourne in 1968. (RNZAF)

In 1950, 18 single seat FB 52s were delivered to the RNZAF, followed by six T 55s in 1952 and six ex-RAF FB 5s. Then, during 1955-6, 21 refurbished FB 5s and five more T 55s were purchased to be used in the fighter, ground attack, and advanced training roles until replaced by the A-4K Skyhawk from 1970.

Top left: Parked at Tauranga on 22 February 1969 Vampire FB 52 NZ5755 displays the unit's red and yellow markings on the fuselage. (RNZAF)

Top right: Vampire FB 5 NZ5765 of 75 Squadron RNZAF high above the clouds during a training sortie in 1967. (RNZAF)

Lower left: When Vampire T 11 NZ5710 and an (unidentified) FB 5 of 14 Squadron RNZAF participated in a flypast in 1972 they had adopted the distinctive 'kiwi' roundels. (RNZAF)

A superbly detailed view as groundcrew remove a 20mm cannon from a Vampire FB 5 of 75 Squadron RNZAF during the late 1960s. (A) is a retractable entry step and (B) is a rubber seal for the canopy (RNZAF)

ROYAL RHODESIAN AIR FORCE

The triple assegai roundels and other details are well shown on Vampire FB 9s, RRAF107 and RRAF 112 of 1 Squadron RRAF parked at Thornhill during the late 1950s. The trailing edge speed/dive brake (A) is fully opened. (RRAF)

Top left: Camouflaged Vampire FB 9 RRAF102 of 2 Squadron RRAF in 1965 wearing the single assegai roundel adopted in 1963. (RRAF)

Centre: With a red flag on its nose indicating it is armed, Vampire FB 9, RRAF112 of 1 Squadron RRAF awaits its next operational strike from Khormaksar, Aden, in October 1960. (author's collection)

Bottom right: Vampire T 11s RRAF130 and RRAF123 of 1 Squadron RRAF during a training flight over the Rhodesian bush in the late 1950s. They wear red nose flashes and fuselage bands. (RRAF)

ADEN ACTION

The Vampires of 1 Squadron, Royal Rhodesian Air Force made regular detachments to Khormaksar, Aden, to assist the RAF with policing the Protectorate. One detachment was in July 1958, as the CO Squadron Leader Charles Paxton recalled: "… we worked in conjunction with the army. When suitable targets cropped up we were briefed and off we went. The first familiarisation flights were up the eastern coast to the Oman border and north along the Red Sea coast where there was a threat from radar controlled Yemeni anti-aircraft guns."

Flying Officer Justin Varkevisser led one of the first strikes up to Wadi Adzzh that was close to the Saudi border, followed by his No 2: "I tipped into the dive and opened up with cannon fire. I started firing all four 20mm cannons with my sight set high above the target and my very first rounds exploded right on target. Flying Officer Randy du Rand led a repeat attack the following day, this time firing R/P (rocket projectiles) at a house sheltering rebel tribesmen that was flattened." Squadron Leader Paxton also recalled attacking these forts: "The first time we attacked one of these forts our rockets went clean through the walls and came out the other side. We discovered that by firing rockets into the base of the fort, we could make the whole thing collapse quite easily."

When Rhodesia was declared a Republic in 1970 the Royal Rhodesian Air Force adopted a new green and white roundel with a golden lion in the centre and green and white fin flashes as shown on these Vampire T 11s of 2 Squadron.

Top: This newly camouflaged dark green/dark earth and silver aircraft had yet to have its serial added when it visited Durban. (D Becker)

Bottom: Vampire T 11 R4201 is readied for flight at Kariba in 1972. (R Johnson)

SOUTH AFRICAN AIR FORCE

The first deliveries for the SAAF were ten FB 5s in 1950, followed two years later by ten FB 52s and six T 55s. These were followed in 1954-5 by a further 30 FB 9s and 21 T 55s that were later used for operational training until withdrawn by 1970.

Main photo: Vampire FB 52 235 of the SAAF Air Ops School 'Bumbling Bees' Aerobatic team at Langebaanweg in 1957. (L Vosloo)

Left: Vampire FB 52 242 in the SAAF 'springbok' roundels soon after delivery. (SAAF)

Below: Vampire T 55 277 of the Waterkloof Station Flight in 1979. (D Becker)

WORLD EXPORTS

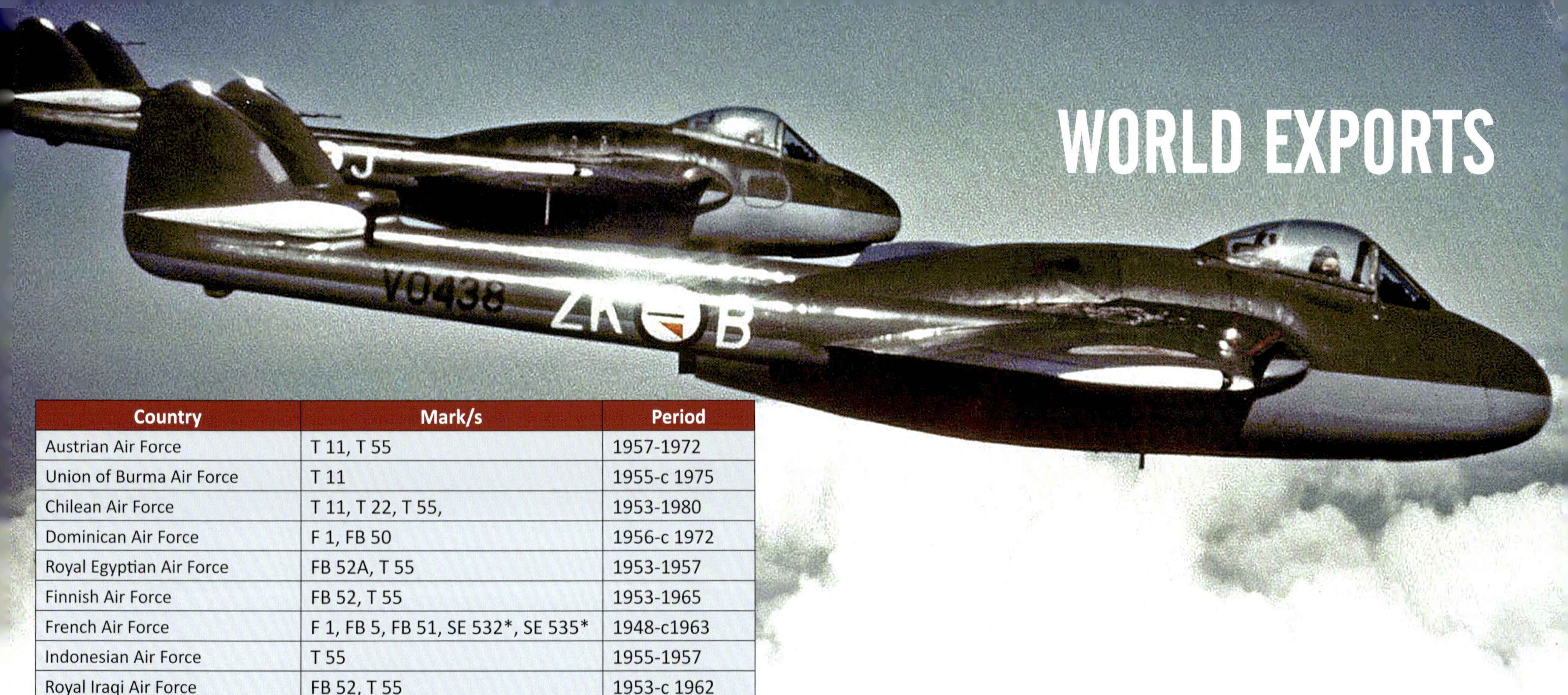

Country	Mark/s	Period
Austrian Air Force	T 11, T 55	1957-1972
Union of Burma Air Force	T 11	1955-c 1975
Chilean Air Force	T 11, T 22, T 55,	1953-1980
Dominican Air Force	F 1, FB 50	1956-c 1972
Royal Egyptian Air Force	FB 52A, T 55	1953-1957
Finnish Air Force	FB 52, T 55	1953-1965
French Air Force	F 1, FB 5, FB 51, SE 532*, SE 535*	1948-c1963
Indonesian Air Force	T 55	1955-1957
Royal Iraqi Air Force	FB 52, T 55	1953-c 1962
Irish Army Air Corps	T 11	1956-1975
Italian Air Force	FB 5, FB 52A+, NF 54	1950-1960
Japanese Air Self Defence Force	T 55	1956-1958
Royal Jordanian Air Force	FB 9, T 11, FN 52,	1955-1972
Lebanese Air Force	FB 5, FB 9, FB 52, T 55	1953-c 1964
Mexican Air Force	F 3, T 11	1960-1970
Royal Norwegian Air Force	F 3, FB 52, T 55	1948-1957
Portuguese Air Force	T 55	1952-1961
Royal Saudi Air Force	FB 52	1957-1959
Royal Swedish Air Force	F 1, FB 6, T 55	1946-1968
Swiss Air Force	F 1, FB 6, T 11, T 55	1946-c1974
Syrian Air Force	FB 52	1955-1957
Venezuelan Air Force	FB 5, T 55	1949-1972

Apart from sales to Commonwealth countries the Vampire was widely exported, eventually flying in the colours of 22 foreign countries, albeit in very small numbers in several cases. The last were retired by the mid-1970s.

Main photo: Although initially unpainted, the aircraft of the Royal Norwegian Air Force were later camouflaged as shown by Vampire FB 52s VO438/ZK-B and ZK-J of 337 Squadron in the early 1950s. (RNorAF)

** Licence produced as the Mistral*

+ Licence produced

NORWAY

Main photo: Vampire F 3s B-AH and B-AE (inset) of 331 Squadron, RNorAF seen over Norway's snow-covered hills in the late 1940s in their early uncamouflaged scheme. The twenty F 3s were later followed by 36 FB 32s and six T 11s. (BAE)

SWEDEN

Above: The first Vampires for the Flygvapnet (Royal Swedish Air Force) were the J-28As (Vampire F 1) such as these of Flot F 3 from Malmen on 27 June 1951. (Swed AF)

Right: J-28B (Vampire FB 6) 'B' of Flot F3 taxies out at Malmen for a sortie in the early 1950s. (Swed AF)

The Royal Swedish Air Force was an early customer for the Vampire. Initial deliveries comprised 70 F 1s (as J-28A) in 1946, followed between 1949 and 1952 by 310 FB 6s (J-28B) and 45 T 55s as the Sk-28C.

Right: The Vampire's diminutive size is evident as Flygdirektör Gunnar von Köhler gets into a Swedish J-28B for a test flight. (Swed AF)

Above: Technicians of Flot F3 work on the Goblin engine of a Swedish J-28 at Malmen in the mid 1950s. (Swed AF)

Left: The first three Vampires, a T 11 and two T 55s, (5C-YB, 5C-Y and 5CYA) are prepared for delivery to the small Oseterreichische Luftstreitkrafte (Austrian Air Force) for jet training duties in 1957. These were followed by three more T 55s and three ex-RAF T 11s and served until 1972. (de Havilland)

Below: The initial Swiss order for the Flugwaffe in 1946 was for an evaluation batch of three F 1s shown here. They were followed from 1949 by 75 FB 6s and a further 100 FB 6s licence built by Pilatus. Also, 42 T 55s were bought by the Swiss Air Force. (de Havilland)

Bottom: Later in their service lives, Swiss Vampires were fitted with an enlarged nose section and some were painted with red and black stripes for the target tug role. (ww2images.com)

FINLAND

Six Vampire FB 52s were delivered to the Ilmavoimat (Finnish Air Force) in 1953, followed by nine T 55s that served for 10 years.

Main: Vampire FB 52 VA-2, HävLv 11 at Pori in 1954 with a black nose number. (Finnish Air Force)

Top left: Vampire FB 52 VA-6 of HävLv 13 at Pori in 1954 has the tail number in blue with a red border. (Finnish Air Force)

Top right: The first Vampire T 55 VT-1 with HävLv 13, at Pori in 1955 with the blue tail number with red border. (Finnish Air Force)

FRANCE

France's l'Armee de l'Air obtained 30 ex RAF F 1s in 1948 for jet familiarization, followed by 94 FB 5s for front line use. Sud-Est then licence-built 187 of the FB 51 and also developed the Nene powered variant named 'Mistral', building 93 SE 532s and 150 SE 535s. Some Vampires also served with the Aeronavale.

Left: Vampire FB 5 VV726/DU-A, VX962/DU-P, VX221/DU-D and others of EC 2/2 'Cote d'Or' from Dijon in 1951. (French Air Force)

Top left: The Vampire FB 5s of EC 3/2 'Alsace' (ex 341 Sqn) like VV720/NL-G retrained the code letters of its WW2 service with the RAF as 341 Squadron. (via R L Ward)

Top right: Vampire FB 5 VX951/2C-D of EC 4/2 'Coq Gaulois' seen around 1950. (via R L Ward)

ITALY

Italy's Aeronautica Militare Italiana received Vampire FB 5s in 1950, followed by a further 51 FB 52A over the next 18 months. Licence production by Macchi and Fiat then saw a further 150 FB 52As, and to fulfil its night fighter requirements 14 NF 54s were delivered by 1953.

Above: The first Italian Vampire NF 54 MM6016 '3-167' on its delivery flight on 28 October 1951, it was lost over the Adriatic en route. (de Havilland)

Left: Vampire FB 52 '4-31' of the 4° Stormo 'Cavallino Rampante' during the 1950s. (G Massimello)

The 3° Gruppo Scuole NAVAR (Nucleo Addestramento Velivoli A Reazione (Jet Aircraft Training Group) at Amendola was a major Vampire user during early 1950s. Its aircraft were identified by the letters 'S-3'.

Main photo: Vampire FB 52 S-3-153. (G Massimello)

Below: Vampire FB 52 S-3-152, S-3-153, S-3-155. (G Massimello)

Top right: Vampire FB 52 S-3-174, S-3-151. (G Massimello)

IRAQ

Six Vampire FB 52s and a single T 55 were delivered as the first jets for the Royal Iraqi Air Force in 1953, followed by six more FB 52s and nine T 55s in 1955.

Right: Vampire T 5 333 seen on 5 June 1953 before delivery to 4 Squadron RIrAF. (de Havilland)

DOMINICA

The Caribbean state of Dominca purchased 25 ex Swedish J-28As (Vampire F 1s) for the Fuerza Aerea Dominicana in 1956, followed by 17 J-28Bs (FB 6s) in 1957. They continued in operational use until the early 1970s. Vampire F 1 2702 heads a line-up of the Escuadron de Caza at San Isidro in the late 1950s. (Author's Collection)